HOME DECORATING BASICS

A Comprehensive Guide
for Home Sewing

HOME DECORATING BASICS

A Comprehensive Guide for Home Sewing

PAMELA J. HASTINGS

Sterling Publishing Co., Inc. New York

A Sterling/Sewing Information Resources Book

Sewing Information Resources

Owner: JoAnn Pugh-Gannon
Photography: Kaz Ayukawa, K Graphics
Book Design and Electronic Page Layout: Ernie Shelton, Shelton Design Studios
Copy Editor: Barbara Paterson
Index: Mary Helen Schiltz

Sewing Information Resources is a registered trademark of GANZ Inc.

Library of Congress Cataloging-in-Publication Data

Hastings, Pamela J.
    Home decorating basics: a comprehensive guide for home sewing / Pamela J. Hastings.
    p.   cm.
    "A Sterling/sewing information resources book."
    Includes index.
    ISBN 0-8069-8455-4
    1. House furnishings. 2. Machine sewing. 3. Interior decoration accessories. I. Title.
TT387.H37   1999
645--dc21
                                           98-46789
                                             CIP

A Sterling/Sewing Information Resources Book

2 4 6 8 10 9 7 5 3 1

Published by Sterling Publishing Company, Inc.
387 Park Avenue South, New York, N.Y. 10016
Produced by Sewing Information Resources
P.O. Box 330, Wasco, Il. 60183
©1999 by Pamela Hastings
Distributed in Canada by Sterling Publishing
c/o Canadian Manda Group, One Atlantic Avenue, Suite 105
Toronto, Ontario, Canada, N6K 3E7
Distributed in Great Britain and Europe by Cassell PLC
Wellington House, 125 Strand, London WC2R 0BB, England
Distributed in Australia by Capricorn Link (Australia) Pty Ltd.
P.O. Box 6651, Baulkham Hills, Business Centre, NSW 2153, Australia

Sterling ISBN 0-8069-8455-4

ABOUT THE AUTHOR

Pamela Hastings is a free-lance author, spokesperson and consultant who has been in the home sewing business for nearly 20 years. As spokesperson for Velcro USA and Waverly she is a frequent guest on decorating and home improvement shows such as Interior Motives and Decorating with Style. Pam also works closely with Husqvarna Viking developing projects for home decorating publications including Woman's Day Specials, Better Homes and Gardens, and Home Magazine.

Pam is also the author of the Sterling/Sewing Information Resources books, Creative Projects for Computerized Machines, Sewing Shortcuts and co-author of Serger Shortcuts.

Pam resides in Wall, New Jersey with her husband Geof and sons Christopher and Connor.

DEDICATION

For Connor Tristan

CONTENTS

INTRODUCTION

 While I always had an interest in home decorating, I really hadn't sewn many decorating projects until I began working as a free-lance person. My first assignments were hosting a home-decorating video for Butterick Company and coordinating decorating editorial features for Viking Sewing Machines, Inc. Although I was involved in these projects, for some reason home fashions still seemed a bit daunting to me.

Shortly after beginning my new career, my family and I moved into a new home and my sewing needs changed. As a free-lancer, I was now working from my home and I no longer needed to sew career wear, but desperately needed to decorate my new home — on a budget no less. A duvet cover, a few pillows and a window treatment later, I was hooked! I still, however, limited my projects to my own home.

Nancy Jewell, PR Director for Viking, suggested that I sew some of the projects for the magazine features myself rather than hiring other sewers. Always hesitant to sew for anyone but myself, I reluctantly agreed to sew an intricate canopy for an editor's apartment. It looked great and I discovered that the key to home decorating is accurate measuring. Once you have measured correctly, the sewing is a pleasure.

As my relationship with Viking and Nancy continues, I always try to make at least one project for each magazine feature. I'll select something I've never made before to challange myself and learn something new. Time and time again I'm pleased with the results and while no project is "goof-proof" (I've had a few unpleasant results!), I'm finding decorating projects are much less intimidating than garments.

Whether you are an experienced fashion sewer or just a beginner, you can easily sew for your home. A few straight seams and you truly can make anything from a napkin to a duvet cover. It's fun to go shopping or browse through magazines and see a beautiful pillow or window treatment and duplicate it at home for a fraction of the cost.

After sewing for my home, friends, and as a business for the past five years, I've realized that whether dressing myself or dressing a home, the satisfaction of making it myself is the greatest joy of sewing!

Chapter 1

WHERE TO BEGIN

Sewing for your home, while rewarding in the end, can sometimes seem overwhelming in the beginning. Whether you are decorating an entire room or just updating with a fresh window treatment and pillow fabrics, begin with a plan.

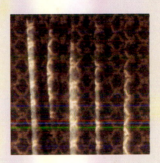

Photo reprint Courtesy of Waverly Fabrics

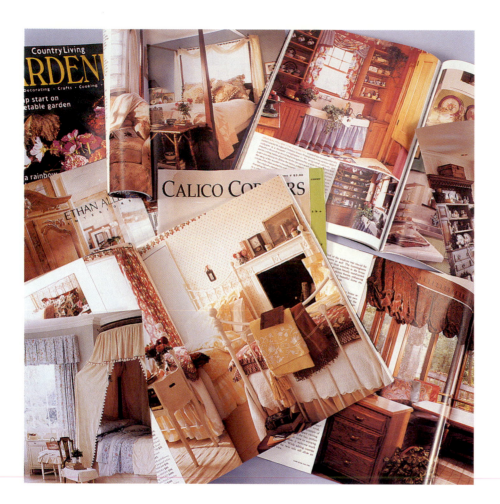

Also visit showcase houses and model homes for decorating ideas. Even the home of your best friend can inspire you in some way. Keep a list of things you have seen in other homes that you like, as well as things you were not overly fond of. The more information you collect the easier your decisions will be later on.

As you plan your decor, you will most likely be drawn to a certain decorating style. Do you favor chintz fabrics in large floral patterns reminiscent of an English garden, or do you prefer country checks and bold stripes? Perhaps you just love rich deep colors and opulent designs for a grand and formal look.

For inspiration and ideas, look through catalogs and magazines, clipping photos of your favorite fabrics, pillows, window treatments, and entire room ideas. Collect anything that appeals to you and place the clippings in folders for each category so they will be easier to locate later on.

As you look through all the ideas you've collected, you are sure to see your personal style emerge. You may find that you have made similar selections time and again. Decorator Amy Riger suggests, stick with what you know and love when deciding on a particular style for your room, because you will be living with your decision for some time. Remember, you are decorating your home for you and your family and you should surround yourself with fabric and colors that are truly "you." It's certainly helpful to be aware of today's trends when planning a new decorating scheme, but colors and fabrics you feel comfortable with are more important than what's hot today.

Amy also says it's okay to live with the same colors or style over and over. It's not necessary to completely change a color scheme just because it's time for new window treatments and slipcovers. If blues and yellows are your favorite colors, by all means use them again in new ways.

When you are ready to begin your decorating process, start a folder with pockets for each room you will be decorating. Your folder should include photos of the room along with measurements of windows and walls. It's also helpful to have the measurements of your bed for duvet covers and dust ruffles. Make a list of all the things you would like to change in the room and prioritize them. If you would like new carpeting but it's not in your budget at the

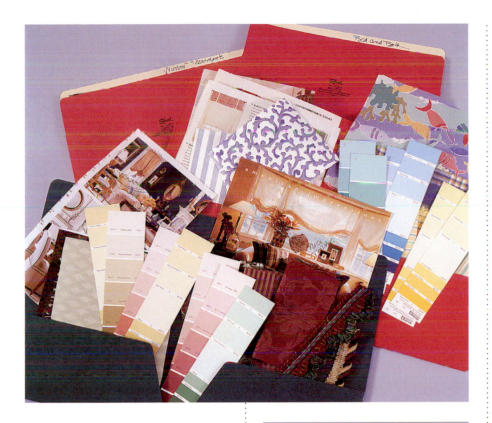

moment, that can go at the bottom of your list; but if you can't live with your walls any longer, painting should be right at the top of your list.

Look through your clipping files and select ideas that you might want to incorporate in your home and add these to your folder. As you begin shopping, add paint chips and wallpaper samples to your collection, as well as fabric and trim swatches. You can then review your folder and choose just the right paint and fabric for your new room.

Once you have selected a main fabric for your decor, trim a piece of the selvage, including a portion of the design, and include this in your folder. The selvage will have a series of boxes in different colors. These are all the colors that are used in the fabric, and this color ledger can be very helpful later on when choosing additional fabrics and accessories.

Remember, doing it yourself is supposed to be fun, so enjoy yourself! If selecting colors and fabric feels overwhelming, consider hiring a decorator to help you get started. Decorators will often work on a consulting basis and give you great suggestions to help you achieve a fabulous look. When it comes to sewing your projects, sew items that you love to make and have time to sew. If your time is limited, consider hiring someone to construct slipcovers or pleated bed skirts and spend your time on window treatments, pillows, and duvet covers.

There are certainly no rules that say you must make everything in the room yourself. The more enjoyable your decorating experience, the more relaxing your room will feel when completed.

Recalling the refined
splendor of great
European estates
and castles, Waverly's
Collection, offers
interpretation of
style – lush tones
architectural
engraved

Chapter 2

FABRICS AND NOTIONS

Decorator fabric as well as some fashion fabrics may be used for home decorating. When selecting fabrics, keep in mind what the end use will be and choose fabrics most suited to your decorating project. For example, upholstery weight decorat-

ing fabrics are obviously more appropriate for covering a chair than a fashion fabric. A fashion fabric, however, would work well as a shower curtain.

Decorator fabrics are generally 54"–60" wide and are treated to resist stains and creases making them the perfect choice for most home decorating projects. Decorator fabrics should be dry cleaned or vacuumed to remove dust; washing may remove special finishes, cause fading, or change the hand of the fabric.

Fashion fabrics such as cottons, eyelet, and muslin may be used for decorating projects such as simple window valances, pillows, or bedding for children where laundering may be a priority.

Mixing various patterns in a room is as fun for some people as it is stressful for others. If you are intimidated by selecting fabrics, shop at a store that specializes in home decorating fabrics. Fabrics are often displayed as collections or in color schemes making the coordinating process a bit easier.

When choosing more than one fabric for a room, make sure you have a balance of prints and textures. Begin with a main fabric; this will be the fabric that you will see the most of in your room. It will usually appear on a sofa or bed or window as these are the largest surfaces to cover. Next select a coordinating fabric; this may be a stripe or plaid in the same color or a small coordinating print from the same collection.

Accent with two or three additional fabrics. If your main fabric is a multicolor print, select a color from the print you would like to accent. Use a solid textured fabric such as damask in this accent color and choose a small all-over print in the same or contrasting color for interest. These additional fabrics will be used for accent pieces in your room such as pillows, table toppers, or even napkins and placemats.

Guidelines to remember:

- Repeat the use of your main fabric more than once. For example, use the main fabric in your window treatment and a chair or table cover.
- Balance your fabric selections. Balance a large print with a small print, a stripe with a solid or small allover print.
- If you cannot decide which fabric to use where, purchase ¾ yard cuts of your main fabric and ½ yard cuts of coordinates and play with them in your room. It will save you costly mistakes in the long run, and these swatches can always be used to make pillows.

NONTRADITIONAL FABRICS

When looking for a unique fabric for a decorating project, there are options other than decorating fabrics. Use vintage tablecloths and linens found at flea markets and antique shops to create one-of-a-kind pillows, table runners, and window treatments. Combine vintage fabrics with contrasting decorator fabrics and trims for beautiful duvets and shams.

Linen tea towels are perfect for creating country kitchen cafés and valances or pillows.

Decorating with sheets is always a popular option. Sheets are wonderful for quick decorating projects. Two flat sheets stitched together create a perfect duvet cover. Sheets are much wider than most fabrics, therefore less yardage is required for many projects. Use sheets to create coordinating bed and bath accessories along with purchased comforters and bed skirts.

When using sheets, bear in mind that if piecing is necessary large prints will be difficult to match from sheet to sheet. For best results, use small prints with a high thread count.

TRIMS AND TASSELS

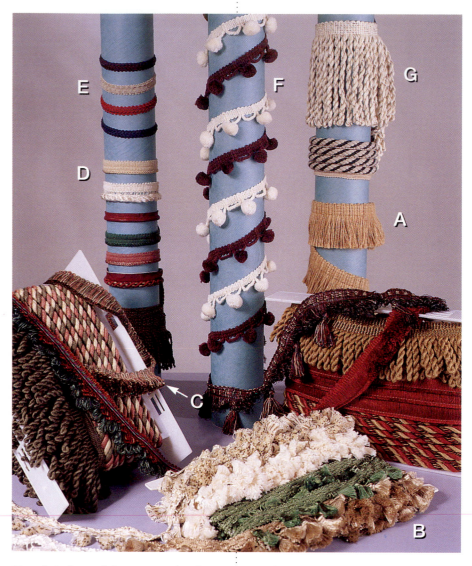

be stitched to the outside edge of decorating projects or enclosed in the seams.

Cord with Lip (D) - A twisted cord is attached to a woven or gimp edging. The edging is enclosed in the seam while sewing, and the cord appears where the seams meet in the same manner as piping. Cord is available in a wide range of colors and textures. Cord may be used for added impact anywhere two seams meet.

Gimp or Mandarin Braid (E) - Flat braid used on the surface of decorating projects is called gimp or mandarin braid. It may be added to lampshades, edges of upholstered projects, or sewn to window treatments, pillows, and tablecloths.

Ball Fringe (F) - This trim is made up of little balls or pompons alternating with loops and attached to a braid edging. Use this trim on pillows and simple window treatments for a country look.

Brush Fringe (A) - Cut ends of cotton or rayon are stitched together to create this luxurious fringe. Most often used as an edging on pillows, the cut edge of the fringe is held together with a chain stitch. After completing your project, remove the chain stitch and brush the fringe for fullness.

Tassel Fringe (B) - This fringe is basically a strip of gimp or braid

with tiny tassels attached to it. The trim may be all one color or have contrasting tassels. Use this trim for pillows and to edge window treatments and table toppers.

Fan Fringe (C) - Similar to brush fringe, this fringe is constructed with loops of rayon or cotton in varying lengths creating a fan effect. It may be attached to decorative edging or gimp and may

Bullion Fringe (G) - This trim is made up of softly twisted yarns hanging down from an edging. Bullion fringe is available in a variety of textures and widths, generally 3" to 9". It may be a solid color or several colors twisted together. Use this trim at the edge of tablecloths, sofas, or ottomans. It may also be used on the edges of draperies and valances. Shorter widths make an elegant edging on pillows.

Tassels (A) - Use tassels at the corners of pillows or square table toppers for an elegant accent.

Chair Ties (B) - These ties are small tassels joined by a length of narrow cording. These ties are used at the back of seat skirts to tie them in place, or they may be used to tie up swags, wrap pillows, or as an adornment on decorative accessories.

Tie Backs (C) - Tassels joined by a heavy cord are called tie backs. These ties are used to hold curtains back in place.

INSIDE SECRETS

Various tapes, cords, pillow forms, and other notions, although not readily visible on completed projects, are essential in construction.

Self-Styling Tapes (A) - Use these heading tapes to create pleats and decorative headings on window treatments. These tapes are sewn or fused to the wrong side of the window treatment and strings are pulled to create the desired effect. Popular tapes include shirring tape, smocking tape, pencil pleat or broken pencil pleat tape, and pinch pleating tape.

Cord (B) - Cord is available in a variety of widths and is used for creating piping and welting to form the edges of decorating projects. Narrow nylon cord is used as the draw cord on Roman or balloon shades.

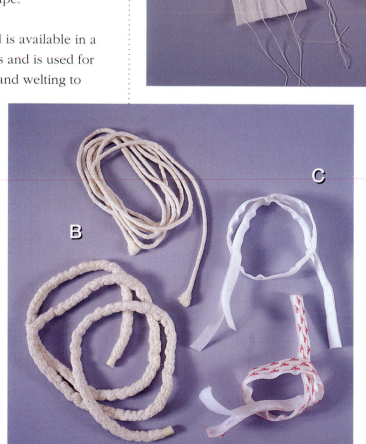

Hook and Loop Tape (C) - Hook and loop tape may be used as a closure on duvet covers and pillows. Use Velcro™ brand Half and Half hook and loop tape for attaching window treatments to valance boards. The loop half of the tape is sewn on to the fabric and the hook portion of the tape adheres to a hard surface for easy installation and removal.

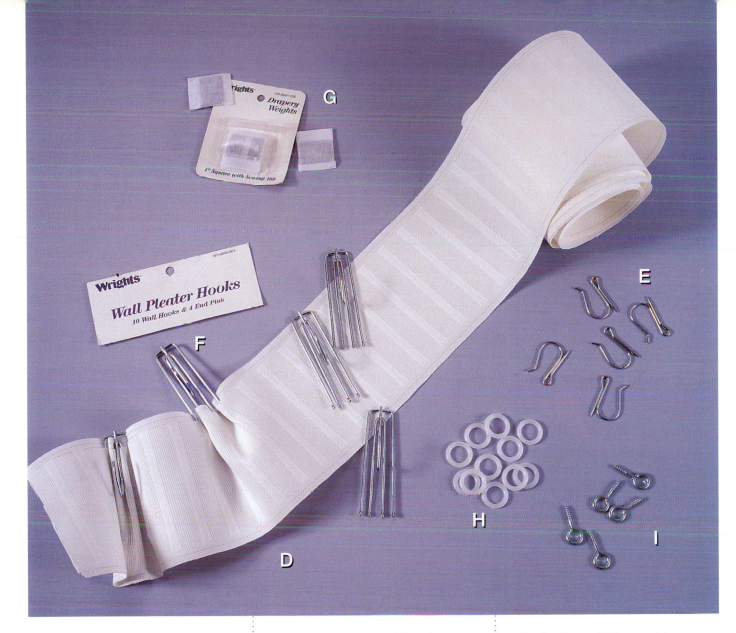

Pleating Tape (D) - This flat tape has a series of long thin pockets on one side. Four-prong hooks are inserted into the pockets to create instant pinch pleats.

Drapery Hooks (E) - Hooks are used to attach pleated window fashions to rings or rods. The pointed end of the hooks is inserted into the fold of the pleat and the curved edge of the hook into the ring or over the rod.

Four-Prong Hooks (F) - These hooks are used in conjunction with pinch pleating tape to create perfect pinch pleats. Prongs are inserted into pockets on the back side of the tape and the hooks attach to the curtain rod or rings.

Drapery Weights (G) - Sewn into the hem of long curtain or drapery panels, weights ensure that the fabric will hang properly.

Plastic Rings (H) - Cord is threaded through the rings and used on Roman, balloon, or other types of drawn shades.

Eye screws (I) - Used to secure the cord ends, eye screws are attached to the mounting board for shades.

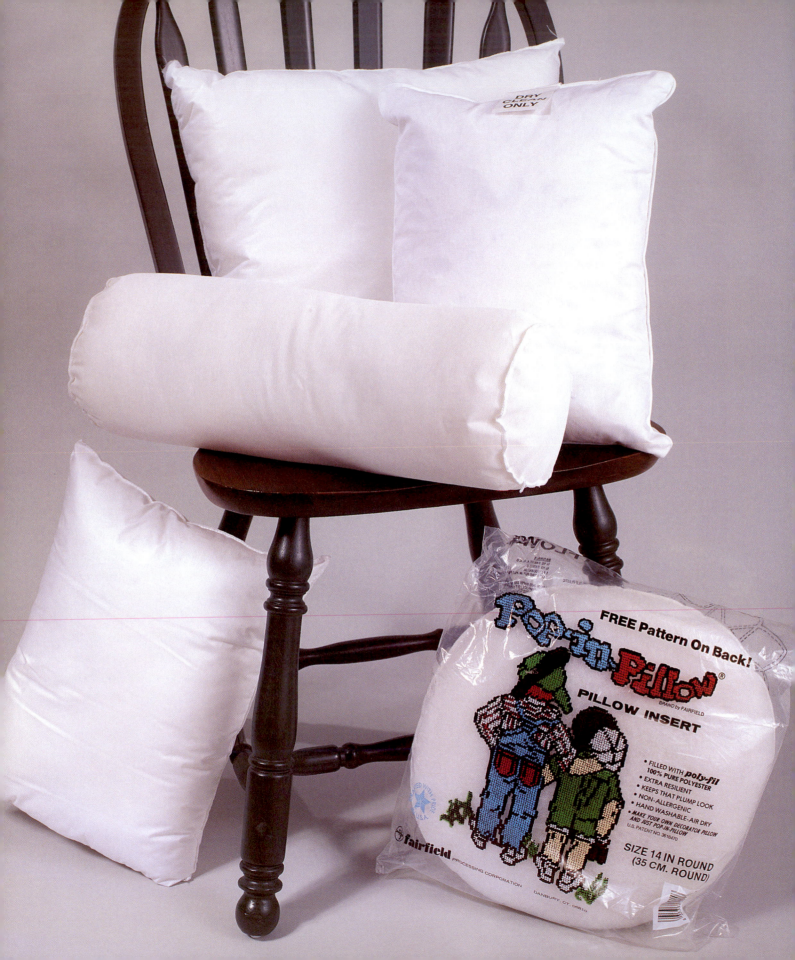

DRY CLEAN ONLY

FREE Pattern On Back!

Pop-in-Pillow®
BRAND by FAIRFIELD

PILLOW INSERT

• FILLED WITH *poly-fil*
  100% PURE POLYESTER
• EXTRA RESILIENT
• KEEPS THAT PLUMP LOOK
• NON-ALLERGENIC
• HAND WASHABLE-AIR DRY
• MAKE YOUR OWN DECORATOR PILLOW
  AND JUST POP-IN-PILLOW
  U.S. PATENT NO. 3616470

SIZE 14 IN ROUND
(35 CM. ROUND)

fairfield PROCESSING CORPORATION   DANBURY, CT. 06810

Pillow Forms - Pillows get their shape from loose stuffing or pillow forms. Pillow forms are available in a wide range of styles and sizes. The most readily available and most reasonably priced forms are filled with polyester fiberfill. Fairfield Processing offers a Pop-In Pillow® form that is firm and a Soft-Touch™ form that has a softer more relaxed look resembling down. Down pillow forms are available at specialty shops, and while they make beautiful pillows they can be a bit pricey.

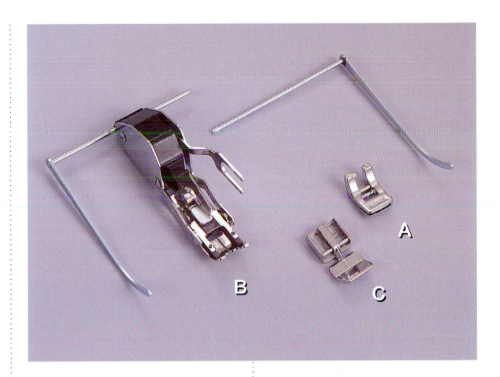

Presser Feet

There are several presser feet available for most sewing machines that are useful when sewing home decorating projects.

The **rolled or narrow hem foot** guides and folds the fabric twice before it is stitched forming a perfect narrow hem. This foot is available in different finished widths based on the weight of the fabric.

The **gathering foot (A)** gathers a single layer of fabric. It also can be used to gather one layer to a flat piece.

The **evenfeed foot (B)** has rubber feet similar to feed dogs on the under side. These rubber feet work in tandem with the feed dogs on your sewing machine to ensure that both layers of fabric feed evenly.

The **zipper foot (C)** may be positioned to either side of the needle so the stitching is close to the edge of the cording, trim, or zipper.

The **piping or cording foot** has a groove on the underside that easily rides over piping as it is sewn. The needle enters the fabric very close to the edge of the covered cord.

Chapter 3

SELECTING HARDWARE

Curtain rods, poles, and mounting boards are
used to install and hang window treatments. The
type and style of hardware selected and where it
is mounted will affect the look of your finished
window treatments.

    The style of the window treatment you select will likely determine the nec-
essary hardware. In some cases, however, the hardware may inspire you to
create a special window treatment. A friend of mine found a pair of unusual
swing rods at an antique shop and was finally able to decide what to put on
her bedroom windows!

When planning window treatments think about how you plan to install them. Be sure there is enough wall space between the outside of the window and a side wall to accommodate large decorative finials. Many of today's new windows have very shallow moldings that make it impossible to mount treatments inside the window frame. Examine your windows carefully to make sure treatments can be hung the way you would like.

Adjustable rods are used to hang stationary treatments with a rod pocket, or casing. Single rods **(A)** are used to hang valances or panels that are held back with tiebacks. Multiple rods **(B)** are used to hang layered treatments such as sheer curtains that hang

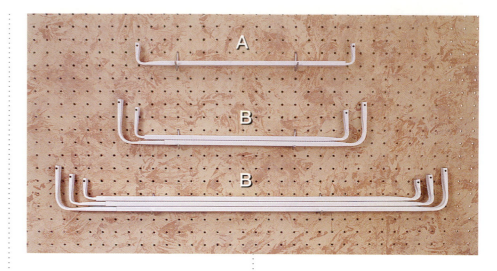

behind draperies or a valance.

Swing rods (C) are hinged rods that actually swing away from the window into the room. They are the perfect rod for windows in small areas that have little wall space around the window. They are also a great alternative to tie backs or draw drapes—simply

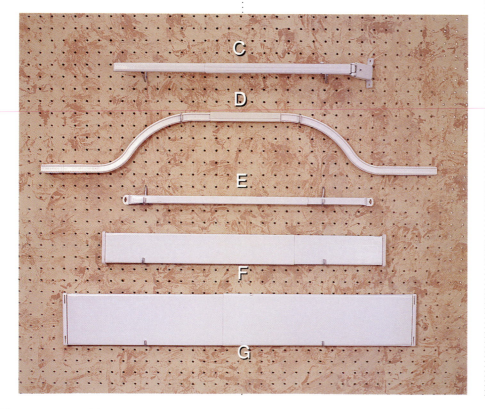

swing open the panels to expose the window.

Mesa rods (D) curve upward in the center to create a unique look for simple rod pocket valances. The rod is inserted into the casing of a straight valance and the valance instantly becomes a shaped valance.

Sash rods (E) are flat rods with a very small (¼") return. These rods are most often used to hang panels that are mounted at the top and bottom of a window like those found on French doors.

Continental™ rods (F & G) are available in two widths, 2½" and 4½", and are used to hang curtains with a wide rod pocket.

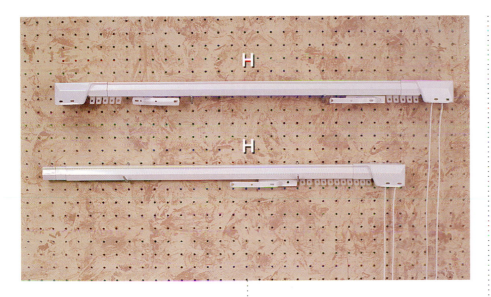

Traverse rods (H) are available in one- or two-way draw and are used to hang draperies that open and close with a cord. With one-way draw rods the drapery panels draw to one side of the window. With two-way draw, the panels open in the center and draw to either side of the window.

Café rods (I) are small brass rods that are generally used to hang lace or fabric panels at the window's midpoint. Café curtains may be hung with clip-on rings, or rings or tabs sewn to the top of the panels. Panels may also have a rod pocket or, in the case of some lace panels, eyelets that the rod may be woven through.

Decorative rods (J) are adjustable metal rods available in a variety of finishes. Curtains or draperies are hung on these rods with rings or tabs. The finials (end pieces) are usually sold separately from the rods so you can create your own unique look. Finials are available in the same finish as the rods, as well as in jewel toned decorative glass or other materials. **Wood poles (K)** are available in a variety of finishes and can be purchased unfinished or painted or stained to coordinate with your decor. As with decorative rods, finials come in a variety of shapes and drapery panels are hung with rings or tabs. Wood poles are often used when draping lengths of fabric for swag window treatments.

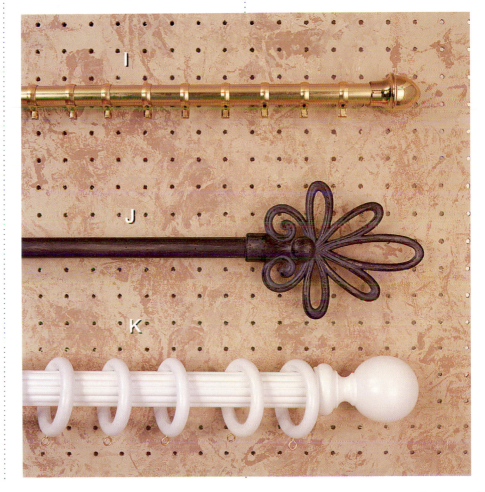

Scarf holders (A & B) are used at the upper corners of the window to hold scarves or swags. They may also be used at the sides of windows to hold draperies back.

Holdbacks (C) are used at the sides of window to hold back draperies and curtain panels. They are used as an alternative to fabric tiebacks or decorative cords.

Swag holders (D) are U-shaped brackets hung in the upper corners of windows. A length of fabric is draped and wrapped around the bracket to create a swag and rosette treatment.

Sconces are used at the upper corner of windows. They are used in the same manner as scarf hold-ers, but have a much more dramatic look and work well with heavier fabrics.

Window treatments do not necessarily need to be installed with traditional hardware. Be creative when planning your windows and think about using ordinary items as unexpected window hardware. An old fishing pole becomes the perfect curtain rod for a simple tab top panel in a den or boy's room. Attach drawer pulls or antique door knobs to window moldings. Valances can be hung with a decorative cord attached at the top or with buttonholes sewn along the top edge. Try using jute cord instead of fabric tabs on panels for an unexpected look.

Mounting boards and L-brackets are used to hang window treatments that do not require a rod, such as Roman shades or tailored swags and jabots. When using mounting boards, cover the board with your window treatment fabric for a more finished look.

Chapter 4

MEASURING AND CALCULATING YARDAGE

Accurate measurements are the key to creating beautiful home decorating projects. Careful measurements are required for ensuring a perfect fit and calculating the correct yardage. When measuring, it is best to use a metal tape rather than a cloth tape measure or yardstick, since a metal tape will not droop or stretch and is much longer than a yardstick.

Draw a rough sketch of your window, bed, or table and record measurements on the sketch. Measure everything twice to ensure accuracy, and measure every window separately even if there is more than one of the same size window in the room. Once you have recorded your measurements, you can sew any decorating project with ease!

WINDOWS

Before taking any window measurements you will need to decide on the specific window treatment style and install the hardware in the desired location.

Hardware may be installed inside the window frame or outside the frame. Poles with rings are generally mounted a few inches above the window frame so the bottom of the ring ends just above the frame. Mount pole brackets on the wall a few inches to the left and right of the window to allow the drapes to clear the window when pushed open.

For basic curtain rods (used in rod pocket drapes), mount the brackets on the wall outside the window with the top of the rod flush with the top of the window or a few inches above the window.

To make windows appear wider, install the rod or mounting board several inches out from each side of the window frame. To create an illusion of a taller window, mount your rods several inches above the window frame.

Once rod installation is complete, you are ready to measure the area of the window that the treatment will cover. This is the finished length and width of the selected window treatment.

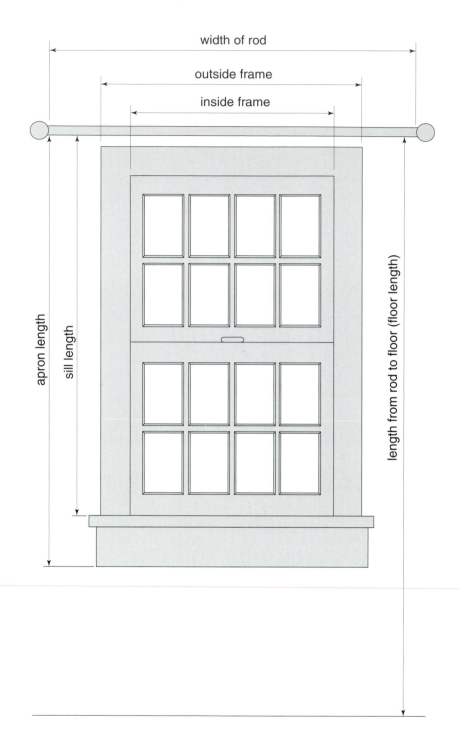

Finished Length. The finished length is the measurement from the top of the rod or the bottom of the rings to the desired length–floor, sill, or apron length. For mounting boards, measure from the top of the board to the desired length of the treatment.

Finished Width. The finished width for inside mounted window treatments is the measurement of the inside of the window frame. For outside mounted treatments, measure the width of the rod between the brackets plus the return (projection of the rod).

Calculating Yardage for Windows

When calculating yardage, use the finished length and width measurements plus allowances for hems, seams, and fullness to determine the cut length and width. You will also need to allow for extra yardage when using printed fabrics that require matching of repeats.
Use the chart below to calculate yardage.

CUT LENGTH

A. Finished length _____ +

B. Add casing/heading (See page 47) _____ +

C. Add hems (See page 46) _____ =

D. Cut length _____

CUT WIDTH

E. Window width x fullness* _____ +

F. Add side hems _____ =

G. Total width _____

H. Total width divided by fabric width _____

*Fullness is the allowance for gathering. On windows this is generally two and one-half to three times the width of the window.

CALCULATE YARDAGE

I. Cut length (D) _____ X

J. Multiply by number of fabric widths (H) _____ =

K. Total length _____

L. Yardage required = (K) divided by 36 _____

TABLES

Tables are measured by adding the dimensions of the table top to a drop length. The drop length is the measurement from the edge of the table top to the desired length. The most popular drop lengths are:

Floor length – edge of table to ½" from the floor

Dining length – edge of table to 1" from the chair seat

Formal length – 18" to 24" drop from the side of the table

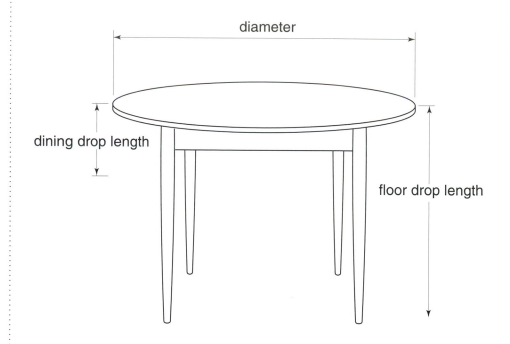

Calculating Yardage for a Round Tablecloth

FINISHED DIAMETER OF THE TABLECLOTH

A. Diameter of table   _____ +

B. Add twice the drop length   _____ =

C. Finished diameter   _____

CALCULATE YARDAGE

D. Tablecloth diameter (C) + hems   _____ ÷

E. Divided by fabric width   _____ =

F. Number of widths   _____

G. Multiply fabric width by diameter (C)   _____

H. Yardage required = (G) divided by 36   _____

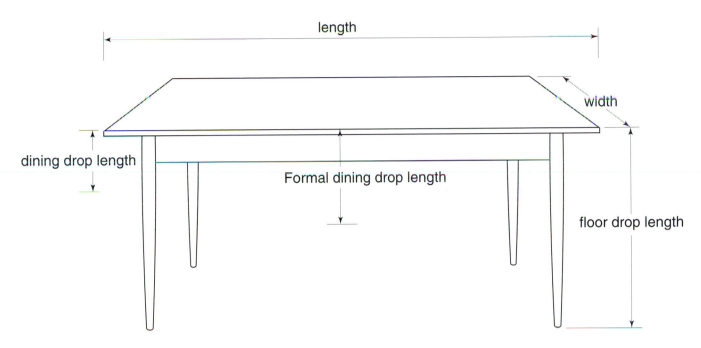

length

width

dining drop length

Formal dining drop length

floor drop length

Calculating Yardage for a Rectangular Tablecloth

CUT LENGTH OF THE TABLECLOTH

A. Measure the length of the table   _____ +

B. Add twice the drop length plus hem   _____ =

C. Cut length of tablecloth   _____

CUT WIDTH OF THE TABLECLOTH

D. Measure the width of the table   _____ +

E. Add twice the drop length plus hem   _____ =

F. Cut width of tablecloth   _____

G. Cut width divided by fabric width   _____

CALCULATE YARDAGE

H. Cut length of tablecloth (C)   _____ x

I. Multiply by number of widths (G)   _____ =

J. Total length   _____

K. Yardage required = (J) divided by 36   _____

BEDS

Although mattresses come in standard lengths and widths, accurate measuring is still necessary and important.

In addition to length and width, drop lengths for comforters or duvet covers and dust ruffles need to be determined. For comforters or duvets, measure from the top of the mattress to 3" to 4" below the mattress line (where the mattress and box spring meet). The drop length for bedskirts and dust ruffles is the measurement from top of the box spring to the floor. Bedskirts or dust ruffles are added to a piece of fabric called the deck which is the length and width of the box spring.

In order to determine yardage for a duvet cover, you will need to measure your existing comforter or duvet. Measure the mattress and the drop length and purchase a comforter that will fit your bed properly. Mattress heights vary as do standard comforter sizes (for example, a queen size comforter may be 84"x 84", 86"x 86", or even 86"x 90"). Check comforter measurements carefully to be sure you are purchasing one with the proper drop length.

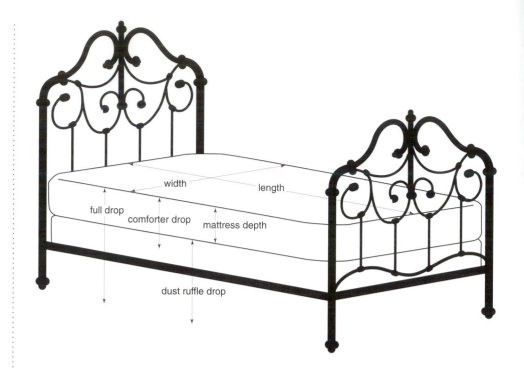

Calculating Yardage for a Duvet Cover

CUT LENGTH

A. Length of duvet plus
    seam allowances   _____

CUT WIDTH

B. Width of duvet plus seam
    allowances   _____

C. Fabric width divided by (B) =
    number of fabric widths required _____

CALCULATE YARDAGE

D. Cut length (A)   _____ x

E. Multiply by number of widths (C) _____ =

F. Total length   _____

G. Yardage required =
    (F) divided by 36   _____

width

length

drop

½" (1.3cm) from floor

Calculating Yardage for Bedskirts

DECK YARDAGE

A. Box spring length plus 1" _____

B. Box spring width plus 1" _____

C. Divide width (B) by fabric width _____

D. Multiply length (A) by width
   (C) = total length _____

E. Yardage required =
   (D) divided by 36 _____

Pleated Bedskirt

CUT WIDTH

A. Measurement from head
   to foot of bed x 2 _____ +

B. Measurement across bed (width) _____ +

C. Add pleat and side hem allowance _____ =

D. Cut width of bedskirt _____

E. Cut width (D) divided by
   fabric width _____

CUT LENGTH

F. Drop length _____ +

G. Add hems and seam allowance _____ =

H. Total cut length _____

CALCULATE YARDAGE

I. Cut length (H) _____ x

J. Multiply by number of widths (E) _____ =

K. Total length _____

L. Yardage required =
   (K) divided by 36 _____

Ruffled Bedskirt

CUT WIDTH

A. Length of bed x 2 _____ +

B. Width of bed _____ x

C. Multiply by 2½" for fullness x 2.5 _____ =

D. Total fullness _____

Continue calculating yardage beginning with step F of "Pleated Bedskirt."

MATCHING PRINTS

Most fabrics used for your home decorating projects will require piecing to equal the required width. When piecing fabric, prints should be perfectly matched along the seamline. When using patterns with a distinct design and repeat, extra yardage is needed to allow for matching.

Calculating additional yardage for repeats

A. Multiply the repeat (distance between repeating designs along the selvage) by the number of fabric widths needed for your project. Round to the nearest ¼ yard.

_____

B. Add this amount to the yardage requirement already calculated.

_____

(For example, if the repeat is 20" and two fabric widths are required for your project, you will need an additional 40" or 1¼ yards (2 x 20" = 40" rounded to nearest ¼ yard = 1¼ yards).

PILLOWS

Measure bed pillows and pillow forms for perfect fitting shams and pillow covers. Very often a pillow form will measure slightly larger or smaller than the label indicates.

Bed Pillow

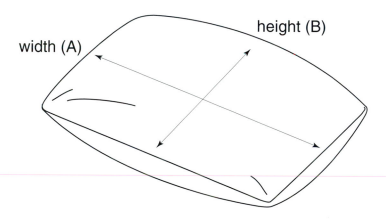

width (A) height (B)

Bed Pillows
Measure bed pillows crosswise from edge to edge to determine the width **(A)** and from top to bottom to determine height **(B)**.

Occasional Pillows
Measure square, boudoir or small rectangular neck pillows as you would bed pillows determining width **(A)** and height **(B)**. Box pillows require an additional depth measurement.

PILLOWS

Neckroll

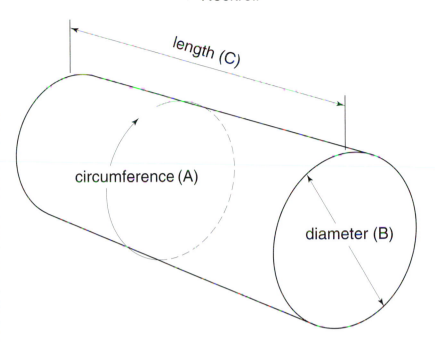

length (C)

circumference (A)

diameter (B)

Neckrolls

Neckroll covers require three measurements. For the circumference **(A)**, measure around the outside of the neckroll. For the diameter **(B)**, measure across one end of the pillow form. For the length **(C)**, measure from one end to the other of the pillow form.

CALCULATE YARDAGE

Average yardage requirements for pillows are:

- 16" square – ½ yard will make two pillows
- 18" square – ⅝ yard will make two pillows
- Standard size flanged sham – 1½ yards
- King size flanged sham – 1⅝ yards
- For ruffled shams, add 1 yard to flanged sham measurements.

Photo reprint Courtesy of Waverly Fabrics

Chapter 5

WINDOW TREATMENTS

Window treatments add the final touch to a newly decorated room. From simple valances to drapes and sheers, the possibilities for the windows in your home are endless. When deciding on just the right look for your home, keep in mind your own personal style and the look you are trying to achieve, as well as the function the window treatment will serve. For example, a room that receives bright sunlight during part of the day would be well suited to window treatments such as butterfly shades or a valance and shutters to block the glare. If your bedroom is drafty in the winter, tab-top or rod-pocket draperies that can be closed will add warmth on cold winter nights.

If you have never tried your hand at window treatments before, don't despair—they are truly as easy as pillows. Sew a few straight lines and in no time you've created a beautiful curtain! Just remember this rule of thumb—always, always measure twice and cut once!

Basic Sewing Techniques

Matching Fabrics

1. Fold the side edge of the fabric under and finger press. Lay the folded edge over the next panel of fabric and match the pattern. Pin in place.

2. Set sewing machine to a zig zag stitch and loosen the tension. Stitch along the fold so one swing of the zig zag just pierces the fold.

3. Turn fabric to wrong side and open out the fold, you will see a ladder formed by the stitching.

4. Using the ladder stitches as a guide, stitch the panels rights sides together. Open seam and press.

Two-Inch Double-Fold Hem

1. Measure and mark a line 2" up from the edge of fabric. Press along the marked line.

2. From the wrong side of fabric, fold the fabric up again and press. Fold the hem back on itself and blind hem or lay flat and topstitch.

Casings

A casing is a pocket formed in the top of a curtain, drape, or valance that a curtain rod or decorative pole is inserted through.

A heading is fabric above the casing that creates a ruffled effect when the panel is placed on a rod.

1. To determine the required depth of the casing, measure the circumference of curtain rod adding ¼" to ½" for ease. To determine heading measurement, add twice the desired depth of the fabric that will be above rod. Add ½" for edge finish.

2. Turn under 1/2" at top edge of fabric and press. Using above measurement less 1/2", measure down and mark. Fold down top edge of fabric to marking.

3. Stitch close to bottom fold.

4. From top edge, measure down and mark one half heading measurement. Stitch along marked line forming casing.

Basic Sewing Techniques

Basic Lining

1. Make a 2" double-fold hem in the bottom edge of the lining, blindstitch or topstitch in place. Repeat with drapery panels. (**Note:** Lining panels should be cut 1" to 2" shorter than the drapery panels.)

2. Press 1" double-fold hem on sides of drapery panels. Open out first fold and stitch drapery weight in place if desired.

3. Align the side and top edges of the drapery panels with the side and top edges of the lining, wrong sides together. With lining side up, turn under and press a 1" double-fold hem in each side edge.

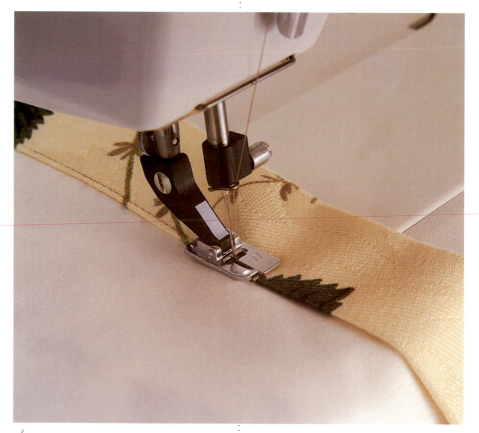

4. Blindstitch or topstitch side-hems in place. Complete top edge based on drapery style.

Simple Lining

1. Cut lining 5" narrower and 2" shorter than decorator fabric. Hem lining and fabric as instructed in Basic Lining.

2. With right sides together and top and side edges even, stitch the lining to the decorator fabric.

3. Turn right side out and press. Two inches of the decorator fabric will wrap around to the back of the drapery panels at sides. At lower corners, tuck under hem of decorator fabric to form a miter and slipstitch in place.

TAB-TOP DRAPERIES

YOU WILL NEED:

- Decorator fabric
- Contrasting fabric for tabs (optional)

CUTTING DIRECTIONS:

- Double the width of the window and divide by 2; this is the finished width of each panel.
- Cut panel the finished width plus 4" by the finished length plus 8".
- Cut facing the finished width plus 4" by 6".
- Cut tabs 3½" wide by the length determined in step 1 below.

2. Stitch a 4" double-fold hem in the bottom edge of the panel.

1. To determine the length of the tabs, measure from the top of the panel, around the rod, and back to the top of the panel.

3. Fold tabs along the long edge, right sides together. Stitch with a ½" seam allowance.

4. Turn tab right side out and press with seam at the center back of the tab.

5. Fold tabs in half, and pin end tabs 3½" in from the side edges, raw edge of tabs even with raw edge of panel. Pin remaining tabs in place equal distance apart; machine baste.

6. Finish edge of facing with serger or ¼" double-fold hem. Pin facing in place over tabs, right sides together, and stitch with ½" seam allowance.

7. Turn facing to wrong side and press in place. Turn under a 1" double-fold hem at each side and topstitch or blindstitch in place.

SCARF AND BISHOP'S SLEEVE CURTAIN

SCARF AND BISHOP'S SLEEVE CURTAIN

YOU WILL NEED:

- Decorator fabric
- Contrasting decorator fabric
- Scarf holders

CUTTING DIRECTIONS:

- Cut decorator fabric and contrasting fabric to measurement determined in step 1 plus 1".

1. Hang scarf holders in desired location at sides of window. Drape string between holders and down window sides to desired length. Remove string and measure. This is the finished length of the swag.

2. Fold fabric in half crosswise, raw edges even. Along one selvage, measure in 18" from the cut edge and mark.

3. Draw a diagonal line from the mark to the opposite corner and selvage. Cut fabric along marked line. Repeat with contrasting fabric.

4. Stitch fabric and contrast, right sides together, with a ½" seam allowance; leave an opening in the top edge for turning. Turn scarf right side out and press. Slipstitch opening closed.

5. On a flat surface, fan fold the scarf. Tie folded scarf in place using ribbon or a scrap of the selvage. Ties should be placed at the portion of the scarf that will go over the scarf holder.

6. Place scarf over holder, arrange pleats and swag, remove ties.

7. Make bishop's sleeve curtains in the same manner as rod pockets, adding 18" to the length.

8. To hang bishop's sleeve curtains, hold curtains just below window sill and tie. Pouf as desired and secure with a hook.
Tip: Place tissue paper or fiberfill in back of pouf to hold its shape.

VALANCE WITH CONTRASTING BAND

YOU WILL NEED:

- Decorator fabric for valance
- Contrasting fabric for band
- Four-inch-wide pencil-pleat tape
- Drapery hooks for hanging

CUTTING DIRECTIONS:

- Measure the length and width of the area to be covered.
- Cut the fabric two times the width of the window plus 1", by the finished length of the valance minus 1".
- Cut the contrasting band to the same width plus 6". It may be necessary to piece fabric panels.

1. Fold under and press ½" on one long edge of band.

2. Pin remaining edge of band to bottom edge of valance, right side of band to wrong side of valance. Stitch in place with a ½" seam allowance. Press seam allowance toward band.

3. Fold band to right side of valance and pin in place. Topstitch close to the fold.

4. Turn under ½" at the top edge and press in place. Turn under and stitch 1" double-fold hem at each side.

5. Stitch pleating tape in place on wrong side of top edge of valance. Place top edge of tape over the raw edge of the fabric and stitch close to the top and bottom edges of the tape. Tie cords together at one edge of the tape, or stitch over cords with a very short stitch length. Pull the remaining cords to pleat; tie to secure and trim the excess cord.

TAPERED VALANCE

1. After piecing panels of fabric, fold fabric in half crosswise, with right sides together. At the fold, measure and mark a point 6½" up from the bottom edge. Draw a curved line from the point to the outside edge of the valance. Use the fabric as a pattern for cutting the lining.

2. Stitch lining and fabric right sides together along upper and lower edges. Turn right side out and press.

3. Turn under and stitch 1" double-fold hems at each side. Attach pinch-pleating tape to wrong side of valance, top edge of tape ½" from top edge of valance. Stitch close to upper and lower edge. Insert pronged pleating hooks.

Basic Rod-Pocket Drapery and Bullion Fringe Variation

YOU WILL NEED:

- Decorator fabric
- Lining (optional)
- Drapery weights (optional)
- Bullion fringe (optional)

CUTTING DIRECTIONS:

- Multiply the window width by two to three times and divide by 2. This is the finished width of each panel.

- Cut each panel the necessary finished width plus 8" by the finished length plus 6" plus heading if desired.

1.Turn up 2" double-fold hem in bottom edge of drapes. Fold in 2" double-fold hems in each side of drapes. Stitch.

2. Fold under ½" along top edge; fold down depth of casing and stitch in place.

BULLION FRINGE VARIATION

1. Before sewing heading in drapery panel, sew bullion fringe to the leading edge of the drape—the edge that faces the center of the window. Pin edge of bullion fringe along side of the panel after stitching hems. Bullion fringe should end ½" from top edge of drape. Stitch in place.

2. Make casing in top edge of drapery panel.

Butterfly Roman Shade

YOU WILL NEED:

- Decorator fabric
- Lining
- Rings
- Cord
- Mounting board
- Screw eyes
- Mounting brackets
- Threaded metal rod
- Connecting screws for rod

CUTTING DIRECTIONS:

- Cut fabric and lining to the width of the area to be covered plus 4" by the length of the window plus 24".

1. Sew fabric and lining together using one of the methods found on pages 48 and 49.

2. Stitch a 1" double-fold hem in the bottom edge of the shade. On lining side of shade, mark the placement of the rings. Make a mark 20" up from the bottom edge and 9" in from each side edge. Make a second mark 3" in from the bottom side edges. Draw a line from these marks to the lower corners of the shade, and a line from this mark to the top edge of the shade. Make ring placement marks every 6"–8" along line. Five

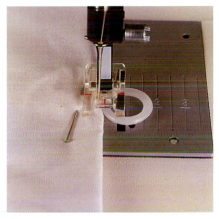

3. Sew rings in place by hand or machine. To sew by machine, set sewing machine to zig zag stitch with a length of zero. Drop or cover the feed dogs. Fold fabric along marking and butt ring against fold. Swing of zig zag should enter fold of fabric and then into the ring. Secure with five to six stitches.

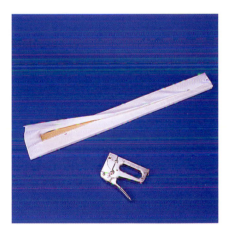

4. Cover mounting board with fabric or lining. To cover, wrap board in a similar manner to wrapping a package and secure fabric with a staple gun.

Reprinted with permission from Country Living Gardner December 1998.

7. With shade right side down on a flat surface, insert screw eyes into the underside of the mounting board directly above the top rings. Run the cord through the remaining rings and through the screw eyes at the top of the board. Repeat with remaining rings. Both cords should end up on the same side of the shade.

5. Finish the top edge of the shade with a zig zag stitch or serger. To attach the shade to the board, lay finished edge of shade on top of the board and secure with a staple gun.

6. Slip cord through bottom five rings and tie together, put a dab of glue on the knots to hold them securely. Work on one side at a time and do not cut the cord.

9. To weight the shade, place a threaded metal rod through the rings just above the five tied rings. Attach connecting brackets to each end so rod will stay in place.

8. To mount shade, attach angle brackets to the wall or inside of the window frame. Place mounting board with shade on top of brackets and screw the board to the brackets. **Tip:** It's a good idea to make pilot holes in the board before mounting.

MOCK CORNICE VALANCE

YOU WILL NEED:

- Decorator fabric
- Lining
- Trim (optional)
- Fabric marker

CUTTING DIRECTIONS:

- Install curtain rod and measure the width of rod including returns. Cut fabric to this width plus 1" by the desired length plus 1".

- Cut casing the width of finished valance by depth of curtain rod plus 1¾".

1. Fold fabric in half crosswise, right sides together. Draw a soft curve at lower edge of fabric. Cut along marked line. Using the fabric as a pattern, cut lining to same measurment and shape.

2. Machine baste the trim to the right side of the curved edge of the valance.

3. Turn under 1/2" on all edges of the casing strip and press.

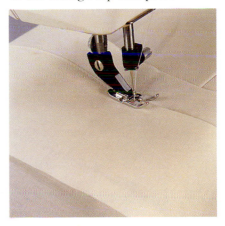

4. Pin casing to right side of lining, 1" from side edges and 1 1/2" from top edge. Stitch close to upper and lower edges of casing leaving sides open.

5. Stitch lining and valance right sides together, leaving an opening in one side edge for turning. Trim seams, turn to right side and press. Slipstitch opening closed.

Chapter 6

BEDROOM DECORATING

Decorating a bedroom is a wonderful way to
experiment with various fabrics. Follow the
guidelines in chapter 2 and select a main print
for your duvet cover and a second print for
the bedskirt. Repeat one of these prints on the

window, and the other on the shams. Choose two to three additional fabrics,

either small prints or textured solids to use for the reverse side of the

duvet cover and for throw pillows. Sewing a bedroom ensemble couldn't be

easier. A duvet cover, for example, is basically a very large pillow case. In

no time you will create an inviting room that will look as though you hired

a professional decorator.

BASIC SEWING TECHNIQUES

One-inch Double-Fold Hem

$1.$ Measure up 2" from raw edge and press fabric to wrong side. Open out fold.

$2.$ Bring the raw edge of the fabric to the crease and press. Refold along first crease.

$3.$ Stitch hem in place close to the folded edge.

Serger Rolled Hem

1. Cut fabric to the exact required length plus seam allowances.

2. Set serger to rolled hem stitch and thread with woolly nylon. Stitch along the bottom edge of the fabric.

Shirring

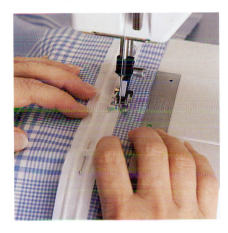

1. Pin shirring tape to the top edge of the wrong side of fabric. Stitch close to each edge of the shirring tape and through one end of the tape.

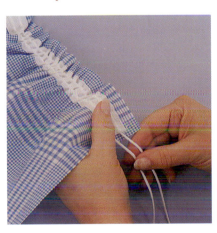

2. Pull on cords to shirr fabric.

Six-inch Box Pleat

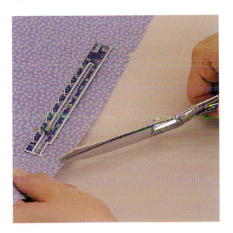

1. Make a clip mark at the location of the center of the pleat. Measure out 6" from each side of the center mark and make additional clip marks.

2. Bring side marks to center mark and pin baste. Press pleat in place. Baste to hold in place.

DUVET COVER WITH BUTTON CLOSURE

YOU WILL NEED:

- Decorator fabric for top of duvet

- Coordinating fabric for underside of duvet

- Ten 2" buttons

CUTTING DIRECTIONS:

- Measure the length and width of your duvet.

- For front of duvet cover: Cut fabric to the required length plus 1" by the required width plus 1" (it will be necessary to piece the fabric).

- For back of duvet cover: Cut fabric to the required length plus 20" by the required width plus 1".

1. To piece fabric for duvet cover, use one full fabric width for the center of the duvet. Divide the remaining width in half, creating two panels of fabric by the required length. Stitch one cut panel to each side of the center panel for front.

2. Piece back of duvet cover in the same manner as the front. Measure 18" down from the top edge of the duvet cover back; press. Cut along the crease.

3. Finish this cut edge with a serger or turn under a ¼" hem and press. Then turn up a 1" hem and press. Stitch in place close to the serged or folded edge.

4. Mark placement for buttonholes on the hemmed edge of the 18" section of the back. Stitch buttonholes horizontally. Overlap hemmed edges and mark

placement for buttons. Sew buttons in place.

5. Stitch the hook side of Velcro™ brand hook and loop tape 1" in from each corner of the wrong side of duvet cover back. Loop side of tape should be sewn to each corner of the duvet or comforter.

6. Button back pieces together. Pin duvet cover front and back, right sides together, around all sides with a ½" seam allowance. Turn right side out, insert duvet, secure in place with hook and loop tabs and button closed.

RUFFLED BEDSKIRT

YOU WILL NEED:

- Lining for deck
- Decorator fabric for skirt
- Shirring tape
- Fabric marker

CUTTING DIRECTIONS:

- Cut lining to the length of the box spring plus 1" by the width of the box spring plus 1".

- Cut three skirt panels, one for each side of the bed and one for the foot of the bed. Cut each panel to the required length plus 2" by two times the required width. (See chapter 4 for instructions on measuring beds.)

1. Make a 1" double-fold hem in the bottom edge and a 1" double-fold hem in each side edge of skirt panels. Sew shirring tape to the wrong side of the top edge of the skirt panels (see "Shirring" earlier in this chapter).

2. Divide skirt into quarters and mark. Divide sides of deck into quarters and mark. Gather skirt and pin to deck, right sides together, matching marks. Sew in place with a ½" seam allowance. Finish seams with serger or zig zag stitch if desired.

Duvet Cover with Tie Closure

YOU WILL NEED:

- Decorator fabric for duvet front
- Coordinating fabric for back

CUTTING DIRECTIONS:

- Cut duvet cover front and back to the measurements of your duvet plus 1".
- Cut two facing pieces 14" deep by the width of the duvet plus 1".
- Cut 16 ties 2" wide by 8" long.

1. To piece fabric for duvet cover, use one full fabric width for the center of the duvet. Divide the remaining width in half, two panels of fabric to this width by the required length, and stitch one panel to each side of the center panel.

2. To make ties, turn under ¼" on one short end and press. Fold fabric in half lengthwise, wrong sides together, and press. Open out and fold each long raw edge to the center crease, then fold in half again; press. Stitch close to the fold.

3. Mark placement of ties along top edge of duvet cover front and back. Baste ties in place, raw edge of tie even with raw edge of fabric.

4. For the duvet back, fold the facing in half wrong sides together along long edge and press. Pin the facing over ties, raw edges even and stitch in place with a ½" seam allowance.

5. Turn facing to wrong side and press. Stitch close to edge.

6. For duvet front, turn under ½" doublefold hem on one long edge of facing; stitch. Stitch facing to duvet front right sides together with ½" seam allowance.

7. Attach hook and loop tape as in Step 5, page 75.

8. Stitch duvet front to duvet cover back, right sides together, along bottom and side edges. Insert duvet through opening and secure lower corners with hook and loop tape. Place top edge of duvet under facing and tie duvet cover closed.

PLEATED BED SKIRT

YOU WILL NEED:

- Lining fabric for deck

- Decorator fabric for bed skirt

- Fabric marker

CUTTING DIRECTIONS:

- Cut lining to the length of the box spring plus 1" by the width of the box spring plus 1".

- Cut three separate skirt panels, one for each long side and one for the foot of the bed. Cut each skirt the required length plus 2" by the required width plus 16". Piece fabric as needed to equal the required width. (Refer to chapter 4 for instructions on measuring the bed.)

1. Prepare the deck (fabric that the bedskirt is attached to, which fits between box spring and mattress) by turning under ½" double-fold hem along the top edge.

2. In each skirt panel make a 1" double-fold hem in the bottom edge and a 1" double-fold hem in each short edge. Make a 6" box pleat in the center of each skirt panel (refer to making pleats in this chapter).

Begin each panel ½" in from the lower corners of the deck. Stitch in place with a ½" seam allowance.

4. Press seam allowance toward deck and topstitch.

3. With right sides together, pin skirt panels to deck, raw edge of skirt even with raw edge of deck.

FLANGED SHAM

YOU WILL NEED:

- Decorator fabric
- Fabric marker

CUTTING DIRECTIONS:

- **For sham front, cut fabric the width of pillow plus 5" by the height of the pillow plus 5".**

- **For sham back, cut fabric the width of the pillow plus 2" by the height of the pillow plus 5".**

- **For overlap, cut fabric 12" wide by the height of the pillow plus 5".**

2. Pin the sham back and the overlap to the sham front, right sides together, and raw edges even. Stitch around all edges with a ½" seam allowance.

3. Turn sham right side out and press. Measure in 2" from finished edge and draw a stitching line. Pin sham through all layers to hold fabric in place. Stitch along marked line.

1. Finish short edge of the sham back with 1" doublefold hem. Finish long edge of the overlap with a ½" double-fold hem.

RUFFLED SHAM

CUTTING DIRECTIONS:

- Cut sham front the width and height of the pillow plus 1".
- Cut sham back the width of the pillow by the height of the pillow plus 1".
- Cut overlap 12" wide by the height of the pillow plus 1".
- For ruffle, measure around all edges of pillow front. Cut strip of fabric two times this measurement by twice the desired ruffle width plus 1".

1. Make ruffle (see "Ruffled Pillow," page 95). Pin ruffle to right side of sham front and machine baste in place.

2. Finish sham back and overlap as in flanged sham. Pin sham back and overlap to sham front, right sides together, and raw edges even. Stitch around all edges with a ½" seam allowance, turn right side out and press.

Chapter 7

PILLOWS

Two squares of fabric and 2 yards of a great trim can be made into a fabulous pillow by even the beginning sewer. Pillows are wonderful learning projects as well as great accessories. Since minimal yardage is required you can really begin experimenting with fabric mixing and matching.

See a print you love, but are afraid it may be too much of a good thing for drapes—pillows are a perfect option. An offbeat print made into a few pillows can really give your sofa that lift you thought it needed. Give your bed a decorator touch by adding a few throw pillows and a neckroll. An assortment of pillows on a window seat creates an inviting cozy nook.

The possibilities for pillows are endless. In fact, you may find the hardest part of making a pillow is settling on which fabric and trim to use!

BASIC SEWING TECHNIQUES

Zipper Insertion

For removable pillow covers, insert a lapped zipper in the side seam of pillows.

1. Using a zipper 2" shorter than the pillow, center the zipper on the seam and mark the top and bottom of the coil. Stitch from the ends of the pillow to the markings with a ¾" seam allowance.

2. Press seam allowance open. Open the zipper and place the teeth on the fold. Pin, then stitch the zipper tape in place.

4. To complete pillow, open zipper and, with right sides together, stitch the remaining edges of the pillow with a ½" seam allowance.

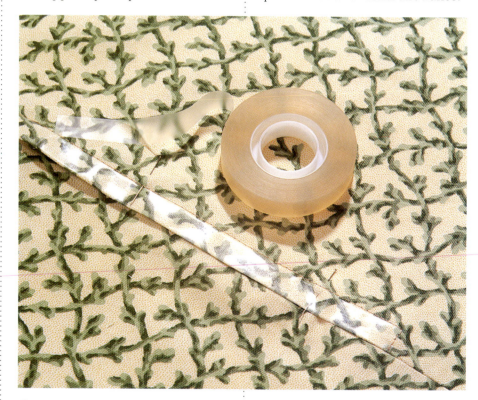

3. Close the zipper and place the fabric flat, right side up. Pin zipper in place through all layers. Place a piece of ½" tape along the edge of the pillow seam to use as a guide. Stitch around the outer edge of the tape.

Piping

Used to accent the edges of pillows and other decorating projects; piping may be purchased or you can make your own by covering plain cord with your choice of fabric.

Shirred piping - Fold bias strip around cord and stitch horizontally across one end to secure. Using a zipper foot, machine baste close to the cord for 3"–4". Leaving needle in the fabric, raise the presser foot and pull on the cord to shirr. Repeat this procedure every 3"–4" until cord is covered.

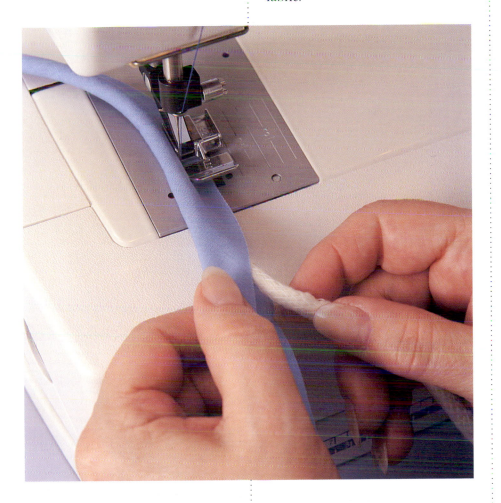

Plain piping - Fold bias strip of fabric, right side out, around cord. With raw edges even, machine baste close to the cord with a zipper foot. To determine the width of the bias strip, measure the circumference of the cord and add 1" for seam allowances.

Basic Sewing
Techniques

1. Machine baste trim to the right side of the pillow, keeping the edge of the trim even with the raw edge of the fabric.

2. Snip trim and hand or machine bar tack to prevent unraveling. Butt ends of trim together and continue sewing.

Hand Stitching

1. Insert pillow and fold under ½" seam allowance, pinning close to the fold.

2. Working right to left, slipstitch the open edges together by taking a small stitch in one folded edge and then slipping the needle through the opposite fold and drawing the thread through.

Tapered Corners

Taper the corners of a pillow before sewing to eliminate "dog-ears," or corners that droop, in a finished pillow.

1. Fold pillow front in quarters and make a mark halfway between the raw edge of the fabric and the fold. Make additional marks ½" from the corner at each raw edge.

2. Draw a line to connect the marks and trim fabric along the marked line. Use the pillow front as a pattern for tapering the corners of the pillow back.

PIPED PILLOW

YOU WILL NEED:

- Decorator fabric
- Cording or purchased piping
- Pillow form

CUTTING DIRECTIONS:

- Cut two squares of fabric 1" larger than pillow form.
- Purchase or make covered piping the length of the outer edge of the pillow plus 4".

1. Pin piping to pillow front, raw edge of piping even with raw edge of pillow. Clip corners as needed. Using a zipper foot, machine baste close to the cord. Begin stitching 2" from the end of the piping.

2. Stop stitching 2" from your starting point and open the piping. Trim the cord so it will butt up against the other end of the cord.

3. Turn raw end of bias strip under and wrap it around the two cord ends.

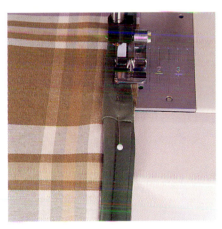

4. Continue stitching. Complete pillow by sewing pillow front and back, right sides together, inserting a zipper or slipstitching as desired.

RUFFLED PILLOW

CUTTING DIRECTIONS:

- Cut two squares of fabric 1" larger than pillow form.

- For ruffle, cut a strip of fabric two to three times the outer measurement of the pillow by twice the desired ruffle width plus 1" (strip will need to be pieced). The ruffle may be cut on the straight of grain or the bias.

1. Stitch the short ends of the ruffle together to make one continuous loop. Fold ruffle in half, wrong sides together, and raw edges even and press. Next, fold into quarters and mark.

2. To gather, set your sewing machine to a wide zig-zag stitch. Place a cord ½" in from the raw edge and zig zag over the cord. Be careful not to catch the cord in the stitching.

3. Pin ruffle to right side of pillow front, matching markings with corner. Pull up on cord to gather ruffle and pin in place. Baste ruffle to pillow front.

4. Complete pillow by stitching front to back, inserting a zipper or slipstitching as desired.

Pillows with Decorative Cording

1. Baste cord to right side of pillow front, edge of cord even with raw edge of pillow. Begin sewing 2" from the end of the cord and stop sewing 2" from your starting point.

2. Remove about 2" of cord from edging. Separate individual cords and secure ends with tape to prevent unraveling.

3. Overlap the ends of the cord so they lie flat and resemble a continuous twisted cord. Pin in place. Continue sewing in the direction of the cords.

4. To complete, stitch pillow front to back right sides together, leaving an opening for turning. Trim, turn right side out, insert pillow form, and slipstitch opening closed. Insert zipper instead of slipstitching if desired.

MONOGRAMMED PILLOW

YOU WILL NEED:

- Decorator fabric
- Fabric for contrast
- Tassel fringe
- Rayon thread for monogramming
- Pillow form

CUTTING DIRECTIONS:

- From plaid fabric:
- For back: Cut one 13" X 17" rectangle
- For front: Cut two 13" X 6⅜" rectangles
- From white fabric:
- Cut one 13" X 6⅜" rectangle
- Trim: Cut two 13" pieces

1. Machine or hand embroider monogram in center of white fabric. Stitch one front plaid piece to each long edge of white piece right sides together using a ½" seam allowance. Press seam allowances toward plaid fabric.

2. Center trim over seam line and pin in place. Stitch close to the outer edges of the trim. To complete the pillow, stitch pillow front to pillow back, right sides together, with a ½" seam allowance, leaving an opening for turning. Turn right side out, insert pillow form, and slipstitch opening closed.

NECKROLL

YOU WILL NEED:

- Decorator fabric
- Ribbon
- Pillow form

CUTTING DIRECTIONS:

- For body of neckroll, cut a rectangle of fabric the circumference of the pillow form plus 1" by the length of the pillow form plus 1".

- For ruffle, cut two pieces of fabric 2½ times the circumference of the pillow form by twice the desired ruffle width plus 1".

- For end pieces, cut two pieces of fabric the circumference of the pillow plus 1" by half the diameter of the end of the neckroll plus 1½".

1. With right sides together, stitch long end of neckroll body. Make ruffle as directed on page 95 and sew one ruffle to each end of the neckroll with a ½" seam allowance

2. Using a serger, finish one long edge of each end piece (or turn under ¼"). Fold end pieces right sides together along short end. Beginning at unfinished edge, stitch with a ½" seam allowance, ending 1¼" from finished end. To make casing, turn under ½" hem at finished edge; stitch in place close to serging.

3. Place end piece over ruffles right sides together, at each end, and raw edges even. Stitch in place with a ½" seam allowance. Turn right side out.

4. Insert ribbon through casings and insert neckroll. Pull up on ribbon to close ends and tie ribbon in a bow.

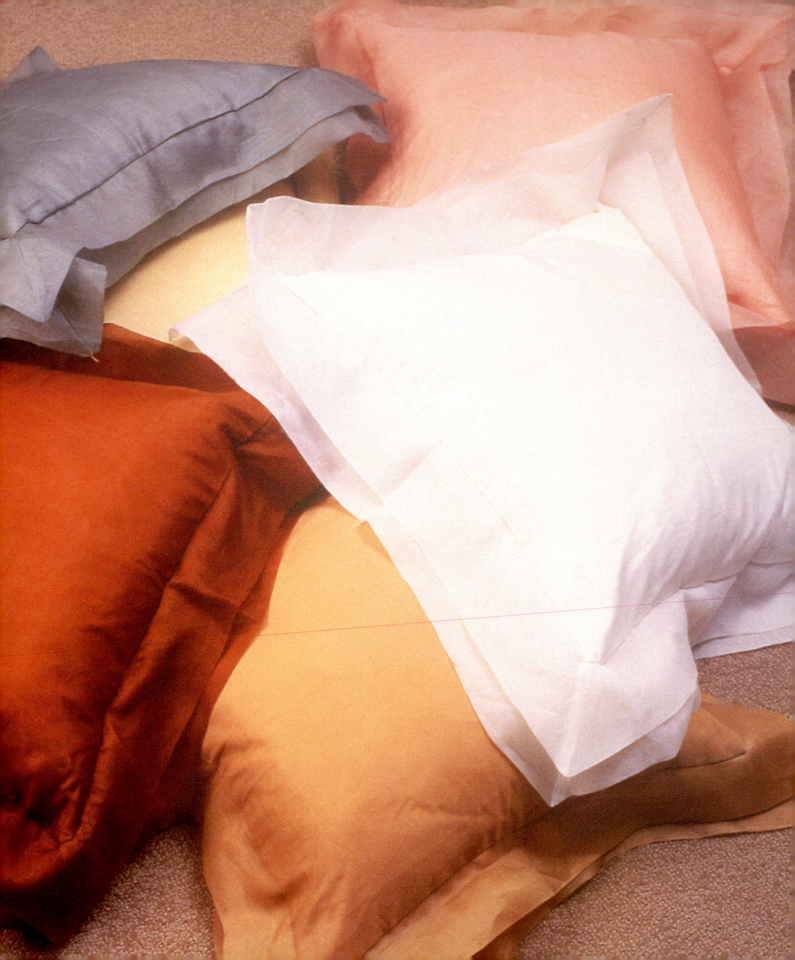

DOUBLE FLANGE PILLOW

CUTTING DIRECTIONS:

- Cut two squares of fabric the size of your pillow form plus 4 times the flange width plus ½". (For a 16" pillow with a 2" flange you will need to cut two 20½" squares of fabric.)

1. On right side of fabric measure the desired depth of the flange and mark. Press flange to wrong side of fabric along marked line; open out creased fabric.

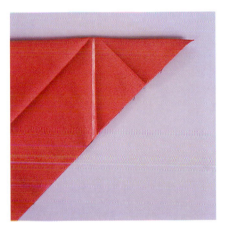

2. Fold fabric diagonally, keeping raw edges even. Fold corner back along short crease mark and trace angle of folded edge.

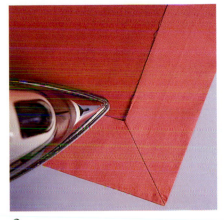

3. Stitch along marked line, trim seam and turn right side out. Press flange in place.

4. Place pillow front and pillow back wrong sides together and pin. Mark a stitching line 2" in from the edge of the flange. Stitch on marked line leaving an opening in one edge. Insert pillow form and machine stitch opening closed.

Chapter 8

TABLE AND CHAIR COVERS

When you think of table and chair covers, the dining room and kitchen always come to mind. Tablecloths in just the right size and fabric are quick and easy to make, not to mention inexpensive! With a minimal amount of fabric

you can create the perfect table for every day or turn an ordinary dining table and chairs into a wonderful holiday party setting.

Custom table and chair covers can add an inexpensive decorator touch to other rooms in your home too. Cover a round table with a floor length cloth and you've added a new accent table to your living room or the perfect bedside table. Give an old chair new life with a bit of paint and a seat cover.

To customize your creations, try adding borders in coordinating fabrics or elegant monograms and embroidered designs.

Photo reprint courtesy of Waverly Fabrics

Basic Sewing Techniques

Narrow Rolled Hem Using Rolled Hem Foot

1. Attach rolled or narrow hem foot to sewing machine. Press under the first 1" of the hem twice and press. Place folded edge under the presser foot and sew a few stitches. Leaving the needle in the fabric, raise the presser foot.

2. Guide the first fold of the fabric into the scroll of the presser foot, holding fabric taut. Lower the presser foot and begin sewing. Continue guiding the fabric by lifting it slightly so it feeds evenly into the foot.

Making a Pattern

1. Place paper or muslin over seat or area to be covered. Trace around the edge with a marker.

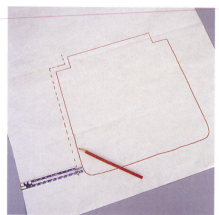

2. Add ½" seam allowance to all edges of pattern and mark.

REVERSIBLE TABLECLOTH WITH CONTRASTING BORDER

YOU WILL NEED:

- Decorator fabric
- Contrasting fabric for band and reverse side

CUTTING DIRECTIONS:

- Cut main fabric to desired size square plus 1".
- Cut contrasting fabric 5" larger than main fabric.

1. With right sides together, sew main and contrasting fabrics together along two opposite edges. Turn right side out and press, so there are bands of equal width on each edge.

2. Turn under ½" on raw edges and then fold remaining edges towards front and pin in place. Miter corners and pin.

3. Topstitch along edges close to the folds and seams.

CHAIR COVER WITH RUFFLED SKIRT

YOU WILL NEED:

- **Decorator fabric**

CUTTING DIRECTIONS:

- **For seat, make pattern and cut out.**

- **Measure around sides and front of seat, cut skirt two times this measurement by the desired skirt length plus 1". Piece fabric as needed.**

- **Cut another skirt piece two times the measurement of the seat back by the desired length plus 1".**

- **Cut four ties 3" wide by 12" long.**

1. Make narrow rolled hem in lower edge of skirt pieces and ½" double-fold hem in skirt sides.

2. Gather top edge of skirt (see "Ruffled Pillow," page 95) and pin skirt to seat, right sides together, and raw edges even. Place ends of skirt ½" in from back edges of seat.

Stitch with ½" seam allowance. Press seam allowance toward seat.

3. Make a ½" diagonal clip into back corners of seat. Fold seat back edges under ½" and over seam allowance of skirt. Pin, then stitch in place.

4. Fold ties in half lengthwise, right sides together. Trim one edge at an angle. Stitch along angled edge and long edge with a ½" seam allowance. Trim seam and turn ties right side out.

5. Fold under and press ¼" on unfinished end of tie. Pin ties to skirt, top edge of tie even with top edge of skirt. Stitch ties in place.

Bistro Chair Cover and Round Tablecloth

YOU WILL NEED:

- Decorator fabric

CUTTING DIRECTIONS:

- Cut chair cover the width of the chair plus 3" by the measurement determined in step 1 below plus 2".
- Cut two side skirt pieces the depth of the seat plus 2" by the length determined in step 1 plus 3".
- Cut 24 ties, 2" wide by 6" long.

1. For chair cover measurement, measure the chair from the floor up over the seat and back, then down the back to the floor. (Tip: Run a string or ribbon over chair and measure.) For skirt length, measure from the top of the side of the seat to the floor.

2. Turn under a ½" double-fold hem in bottom and side edges of skirt. Make ½" double-fold hem in short edges of chair cover.

3. Place cover over chair and mark front and back edges of seat.

4. Pin top edge of skirt to chair cover between markings, wrong sides together. Machine baste in place.

5. Turn under and stitch ½" double-fold hem in side of chair cover. Top edge of skirt will be folded in to this hem.

6. Make ties as described in "Duvet Cover with Tie Closure," page 79.

7. Place cover over chair and mark placement of ties. There will be two ties on each skirt edge and two ties on each back edge. Stitch ties in place at marks.

ROUND TABLECLOTH

CUTTING DIRECTIONS:

- **Measure the diameter of the table and the desired drop length (see chapter 4 for instructions on measuring tables). Cut fabric the diameter of the table plus twice the drop length plus 1" for hems. If the diameter of the tablecloth is wider than the fabric width, piecing will be necessary.**

1.Stitch fabric panels together to create a large square. Sew panels so that there is one fabric width in the center and two side panels.

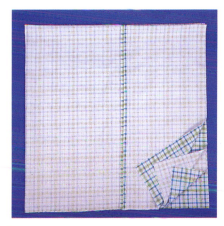

2. Fold fabric in half lengthwise and then crosswise into quarters, matching raw edges. Pin through all layers to hold fabric in place.

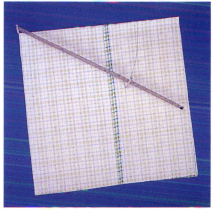

3. Cut a piece of string to half the diameter of the tablecloth and tie a marker to one end. Pin end of string to folded corner of tablecloth and mark outer edge of circle (or use a yardstick compass as we have used here). Cut along marked line.

4. Hem with a narrow hem or serger rolled hem.

PLAID TABLE TOPPER

CUTTING DIRECTIONS:

- Cut a square of fabric to the desired size for table.

1. One method for finishing edges on table toppers is with a rolled hem using an overlock machine. Dab seam sealant in the corners before trimming the chain.

2. An alternative method is to finish edges of table topper with a double fold hem. Turn under and press a ½" double fold hem on each edge of topper.

3. Unfold one edge completely and the adjoining edge half way. Turn corner of fabric in diagonally and press.

4. Refold edges to create a mitered corner.

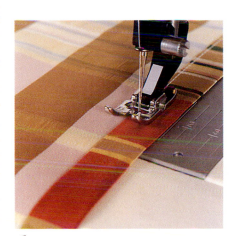

5. Topstitch hem in place close to fold.

EMBROIDERED TABLE TOPPER

YOU WILL NEED:

- Decorator fabric
- Contrasting fabric for band
- Rayon thread for embroidery
- Embroidery card (for embroidering by machine)
- Fabric marker

CUTTING DIRECTIONS:

- Cut fabric as directed for round tablecloth
- Cut bias band of contrasting fabric the circumference of the tablecloth by 2" wide.

1. Stitch fabric together and cut into circle as directed in step 1 of the "Round Tablecloth" instructions, page 113.

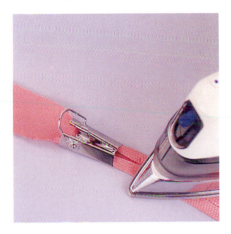

2. Run bias band through a bias strip maker and press raw edges to center.

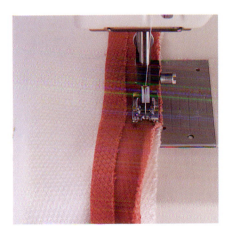

3. Open out one raw edge of bias band. Pin right side of band to wrong side of tablecloth. Stitch in place with a ½" seam allowance. Trim seam.

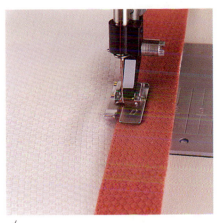

4. Fold band to right side of tablecloth, and press in place. Pin edge in place and stitch close to the fold.

5. Mark placement of embroidery motif on right side of tablecloth. Embroider motif by hand or machine following embroidery or machine instructions.

FITTED CHAIR COVER

Courtesy of Viking Sewing Machine Co.

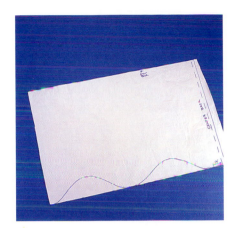

1. Measure around edge of entire seat adding 4". On pattern paper draw a skirt the desired length, by the seat measurement. At one short edge of the pattern, mark a ½" seam allowance. At the top of pattern, mark the back corner of seat. At bottom of pattern, measure in 4" from short edge and mark. Draw a scallop along bottom edge of pattern. The midpoint of the scallop should begin at lower edge mark. Cut skirt from fabric and lining.

2. Sew skirt and lining, right sides together, along short edges and from top mark to short edge. Clip

at mark. Trim seam, turn right side out and press. Baste along top and bottom edges.

3. Make bias tape using a bias tape maker. (See embroidered tablecloth on page 117.) Fold bias tape in half lengthwise and press. Enclose curved edge of chair skirt with tape and pin in place. Press tape easing along curve as needed.

4. Stitch bias tape in place close to fold. Make sure to catch top and bottom edges as you sew.

5. Mark placement of buttonholes along right side of the right-hand end of skirt. Stitch buttonholes.

6. Stitch seat and seat lining together along the back edge only. Trim seam, turn right side out and press. Pin skirt to seat, matching marks. Stitch in place with a ½" seam allowance. Finish seam with an overlock or zigzag stitch.

FITTED TABLECLOTH

CUTTING DIRECTIONS:

- For tablecloth top, cut fabric to length and width of the top of the table plus 1".
- For skirt, cut fabric the measurement of all four sides of the table plus 1", by the desired drop length plus 1" (fabric will need to be pieced).

1. Fold tablecloth top into quarters. Using a small plate or cup, mark a curve in the corner of the fabric where the raw edges meet. Cut along marked line.

2. Baste cord to edge of top, the edge of the piping even with the edge of the fabric.

3. Join short ends of skirt to create a continuous piece of fabric. Make a narrow hem in the bottom edge of the skirt.

4. Pin the skirt to the top, right sides together; clip as needed at the corners.

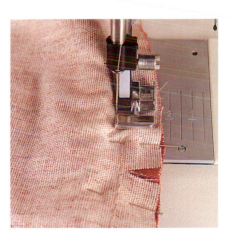

5. With right side of top down, stitch skirt to top just inside the piping basting line.

Measurement Charts

Standard Measurements for Mattresses

Twin	39" x 75"
Full	54" x 75"
Queen	60" x 80"
King	76" x 80"

Bed Pillow Measurements

Standard	20" x 28"
Queen	20" x 30"
King	20" x 36"
Euro	26" x 26"

Standard Measurements for Duvet Fillers *

Twin	64" x 86"
Full	74" x 86"
Queen	84" x 90"
King	100" x 88"

*The above are standard measurements. If you are making a duvet cover for an existing comforter, measure your filler exactly as there may be a slight variation from the above measurements.

Continuous Bias (from one yard of fabric to the nearest yard)

		Bias Strip Width			
		1 1/4"	1 3/4"	2 1/4"	2 3/4"
Fabric Width	54"	35 yds	25 yds	19 yds	16 yds
	60"	47 yds	34 yds	26 yds	21 yds

Determine the yield of bias strip from a given amount of fabric using the following calculation:

1. Multiply the length times the width

2. Divide this result by the desired bias width

3. Divide again by 36

METRIC EQUIVALENTS

Inches to Millimeters and Centimeters
MM - millimeters   CM - centimeters

Inches	MM	CM	Inches	CM	Inches	CM
⅛	3	0.3	9	22.9	30	76.2
¼	6	0.6	10	25.4	31	78.7
⅜	10	1.0	11	27.9	32	81.3
½	13	1.3	12	30.5	33	83.8
⅝	16	1.6	13	33.0	34	86.4
¾	19	1.9	14	35.6	35	88.9
⅞	22	2.2	15	38.1	36	91.4
1	25	2.5	16	40.6	37	94.0
1¼	32	3.2	17	43.2	38	96.5
1½	38	3.8	18	45.7	39	99.1
1¾	44	4.4	19	48.3	40	101.6
2	51	5.1	20	50.8	41	104.1
2½	64	6.4	21	53.3	42	106.7
3	76	7.6	22	55.9	43	109.2
3½	89	8.9	23	58.4	44	111.8
4	102	10.2	24	61.0	45	114.3
4½	114	11.4	25	63.5	46	116.8
5	127	12.7	26	66.0	47	119.4
6	152	15.2	27	68.6	48	121.9
7	178	17.8	28	71.1	49	124.5
8	203	20.3	29	73.7	50	127.0

METRIC CONVERSION CHART

Yards	Inches	Meters	Yards	Inches	Meters
⅛	4.5	0.11	1 ⅛	40.5	1.03
¼	9	0.23	1 ¼	45	1.14
⅜	13.5	0.34	1 ⅜	49.5	1.26
½	18	0.46	1 ½	54	1.37
⅝	22.5	0.57	1 ⅝	58.5	1.49
¾	27	0.69	1 ¾	63	1.60
⅞	31.5	0.80	1 ⅞	67.5	1.71
1	36	0.91	2	72	1.83

ACKNOWLEDGMENTS

Thank you to the following companies for providing the use of their products:

Kirsch Drapery Hardware – all curtain rods and hardware
For information (800) 528-1407

Calico Corners – fabric for valance with band, rod-pocket drapes, tab-top curtains, and pillow with twisted cord. Waverly fabrics available at Calico Corners.
For information (800) 213-6399

Waverly – fabric; archive photography.
For information (800) 556-0040

Hollywood Trims by Dritz – trims

Husqvarna Viking Sewing Machine Company – sewing machine products
For information (800) 358-0001

Fairfield Processing Corporation – pillow forms

Velcro USA – Velcro™ Soft & Flexible

Additional photography – Brian Kraus Photography; Jeffrey Gross Photography; Paul Whicheloe

Special thanks to JoAnn for all her assistance and for letting me do this book, and to Barbara Patterson for a wonderful editing job.

INDEX

Index

INDEX

INDEX